MEMORIAL DAY WITH
Granddaddy Meek

Whitney White
Illustrated by Kim Merritt

A Different Kind of Day

As the car pulled into Mama D and Granddaddy Meek's driveway, Brennan and Addison couldn't believe their eyes. The massive, old oak trees that surrounded the house were bending and swaying like young saplings. Limbs littered the yard and leaves swirled throughout the air. The dark, sunless morning sky and the rumbling thunder gave the children an anxious feeling as they unbuckled their seatbelts.

"You kids pay attention to the weather today," Dad said as he put the car in park.

"We will," Addison replied, watching Mama D's pampered flowers struggle to stay rooted through the gusts of wind.

"Are you sure you want to stay? You can come with us if you're worried about the weather," Mom offered nervously.

"We'll be fine," Brennan said confidently. "Granddaddy Meek and Mama D may need us today."

Dad looked surprised. "This sure is a change from last week when you begged us not to leave you here!"

"Well, Mom was actually right," Addison answered. "We like staying in Covenant Creek!"

Mom smiled. "I'm glad you do. Please be on your best behavior. Help Mama D and don't bother Granddaddy Meek!"

Without warning, thunder boomed, causing the coins in the cupholders to rattle. "We better go before it rains!" shouted Addison as she and Brennan pushed the car door open and ran as fast as they could.

Before driving away, their parents watched in disbelief as the siblings willingly ran through a brewing storm to get to that front porch. Since Mom and Dad worked during the summer, Granddaddy Meek and Mama D had been the only option for the children to stay with once the school year ended. As a child, Mom spent every summer in Covenant Creek, and she felt sure the simple country life would be a great learning experience for her city kids. Brennan and Addison, on the other hand, had been furious about being stranded in the country with their great-grandparents and no wi-fi for an entire summer.

However, much to their surprise, they instantly fell in love with the peaceful summer days in Covenant Creek. They freely explored the woods, jumped hay bales, fed farm animals, and even built a fort in an abandoned barn. They drank sweet tea when they were hot, ate peaches right off the tree when they needed a snack, and proudly wore dirt on their clothes. There were no other children around for miles, but they quickly became friends with most all of the sweet elderly people in the tiny community.

The only person they weren't quite friends with yet was their mysterious Granddaddy Meek. Brennan and Addison had been terrified of him for as long as they could remember. He had always seemed angry, irritable, and unusually quiet. So, they were very careful to stay out of his way and avoid eye contact at all costs. That was their plan when Mom arranged for them to stay in Covenant Creek, but on their very first day at his house, he caught them snooping in his closet!

Trembling and fearing for their lives that day, he did something they couldn't believe. Instead of losing his temper like they expected, he patiently took the time to teach them about the special American symbols he kept in the treasure chest they were prying in. He also shared with them a few details of his experience in World War II, like seeing the first American flag ever flown on Japanese soil. Until then, they had never even known he was a soldier!

Ever since that day, they had been fascinated by his heroism and eager to learn more about him. But for some reason, he never seemed to enjoy their endless questions as he tried to relax on the front porch. It usually didn't take long for him to escape and find anything else to do once they found him and bombarded him with chatter. Yet, they still felt sure that deep down in his heart, way deep down, he was delighted to have them around. Their friendship was definitely a work in progress.

Without fail, every morning since Mom began dropping them off, Granddaddy Meek was always sitting on the front porch when they arrived. They would happily run to greet him and without the slightest smile, he'd say, "Mornin'," nod his head, and look the opposite direction. But today was different.

As they reached the front porch and waved goodbye to their parents through the strange weather, Brennan immediately noticed the empty chair. "Hey, where's Granddaddy Meek?"

Brushing her blowing hair from her face, Addison turned to look for him. "That's weird. He's always here."

"Look!" Brennan said, pointing to the flag pole in the front yard. "I've never seen his flag look like that before.

I wonder if he forgot to raise it the rest of the way or if he just decided it was too stormy."

"Maybe he doesn't feel good today," Addison replied. "Come on. He's probably waiting for us inside."

No sooner than Addison opened the door, the smell of Mama D's big breakfast led them to the kitchen, but there was also a different smell.

"We're here, Mama D!" Brennan announced.

Mama D dried her hands on her apron and smiled as she gladly hugged them both.

"What's that good smell?" Addison asked hungrily.

Mama D pointed to the stove. "Fresh apple pies!"

"Oh, I can't wait to taste them!" Brennan exclaimed, staring at the perfect golden crusts.

"Come now, breakfast is ready," Mama D said, leading them to the table and away from the tempting pies.

After blessing the food, she read to them from her tiny devotion book as she did every morning. Then Brennan and Addison raced to pile pancakes and bacon high on their plates as Mama D poured homemade hot chocolate into their cups.

Suddenly, they heard the bedroom door close, then the steady thud-bump…thud-bump coming down the hall. It was the same noise they had heard while they fearfully hid in Granddaddy Meek's closet the day they were snooping. Though they were no longer startled by it, it was a sound they would remember the rest of their lives – the sound of Granddaddy Meek's distinct, heavy limp when he walked. Neither one of

them had ever been brave enough to ask him what happened, but it was a mystery they were determined to solve one day… when they worked up enough courage.

"Morning, Granddaddy Meek!" Addison said cheerfully as he entered the room. "You look different today!"

He said nothing. Instead, he slowly eased down in his seat and began to read the newspaper.

"It's a good different," she continued, unbothered by his silence. "You look nice. You even smell nice, too!"

Granddaddy Meek grunted and kept reading the newspaper.

"Oh, Granddaddy Meek," Brennan said between bites of bacon, "we noticed your flag. Did you forget to raise it all the way?"

Granddaddy Meek dropped his newspaper to look Brennan in the eye. "Delores, did you hear that boy?"

"Drink your coffee, honey," Mama D replied patiently as she placed his fresh coffee in front of him.

The warm wind blew through the open windows, stirring the uncomfortable awkwardness. Brennan didn't understand what he had said that was wrong or why Granddaddy Meek was acting more gruff than usual. So, he tried to cheer him up by saying, "Hey, the good news is Mama D fixed pies for us! That'll make you feel better."

With that, Granddaddy Meek flung his newspaper on the table causing the dishes to clang. "Make me feel better?" he snapped. "Son, those pies aren't for me and they certainly aren't for you."

Granddaddy Meek's chair screeched across the floor as he stood abruptly, steadying himself with the kitchen counter. Addison noticed a large, unfamiliar picture by his hand.

"Wait, Granddaddy Meek! Who's the soldier in that picture?" Addison asked innocently. "I've never seen that guy before."

At once, Granddaddy Meek's hardened face looked heartbroken as he paused to ponder the picture. Brennan didn't like seeing him sad. Again, he persistently tried to change the subject to ease the tension. "Guess what, Granddaddy Meek? Today is a special day!"

Granddaddy Meek shifted his gaze from the picture to Brennan. With a hopeful voice, he asked, "Is that right? Tell me what's special about today."

"It's the first day of summer!" Brennan said excitedly. "Mom and Dad brought us here today so they could go get groceries and prepare for our big cookout celebration tonight. I hate that the weather is bad, but it won't ruin our fun. I love this holiday!"

Granddaddy Meek's jaw clenched. He swiped his veteran hat from the table in anger and accidentally knocked over his coffee cup making the children jump. "I've heard enough. I think it's best I head to town now. You kids get a rag and clean this mess up for Mama."

Brennan and Addison were shocked. Although he had always seemed angry, this was a side of him they had never actually witnessed before.

This was a different kind of day. Very different.

A Bumpy Ride

"I declare!" Mama D exclaimed as she and the children cleaned the spilled coffee. "He left the pies! Hurry, children, catch him before he leaves."

With no hesitation, they grabbed the pies and raced outside under the dreary sky. Granddaddy Meek was nearly out of the driveway when he noticed them. The gravel under his tires crunched as his brakes halted hastily. Scowling, he waited for Brennan and Addison to bring the pies to his old, rusty pickup truck as the thunder growled and the wind whipped.

"I could go with you since the weather's bad, Granddaddy Meek. Do you need help?" Brennan asked as Granddaddy Meek reached for the pies through the truck window.

"No, son, I believe you've done enough," Granddaddy Meek said sternly.

"Now, Dennis, you should be ashamed of yourself. Let those children go with you!" Mama D demanded as she caught up with them.

The children were surprised by her tone, and from the look on Granddaddy Meek's face, he was, too.

"Not today, dear," he said politely, but firmly.

She put her hands on her hips. With gentleness in her voice and boldness in her words, she insisted clearly over the wind, "Yes, today! If you don't teach them, then who will?"

Granddaddy Meek seemed to soften as he looked at her, but as his eyes turned back toward Brennan and Addison, his sourness returned. "Get in the truck," he said in defeat.

Though they knew he was upset, Brennan and Addison were thrilled that he was actually letting them go. They fought back smiles as they scurried to the passenger side and quietly climbed in the truck.

For ten miles into town, the only sounds that could be heard were the crackles of thunder and the creaks and squeaks of the beat-up truck bouncing along the bumpy country roads. Finally, Granddaddy Meek pulled into a parking lot with only one other old, beat-up truck. "Stay here," he ordered.

The siblings studied the old, brick building as he carefully limped in. "What is this place?" Brennan asked.

"I'm not sure," Addison said looking around. "Wait! There's a sign. It says, 'V-F-W. Veterans of Foreign Wars.'"

Excitedly, Brennan whispered, "Oh, maybe this is a secret club for veterans! He probably meets here with his old war buddies. I bet they still work undercover on top secret war missions. That's probably why he's in a bad mood. He's just stressed. Makes perfect sense."

Addison rolled her eyes. Her brother had a wild imagination. "That's crazy. Everyone knows veterans take care of animals. I'm sure this is a hospital for animals that have been hurt in foreign wars, but it's odd that Granddaddy Meek would be here. He doesn't seem to be a pet lover."

All of a sudden, the door of the building swung open. Granddaddy Meek made his way back to the truck carrying a large box. "Hold these," he said as he plopped the box on Brennan's lap and slid in the driver's seat.

"Flowers!" Addison squealed as she peeked in the box. "This is a flower shop, too?"

"Flower shop?" he questioned angrily. "Don't you have any idea what today is?"

"Yes, sir, it's Monday," Brennan said with assurance.

"Just another Monday, huh?" Granddaddy Meek asked bitterly. "I guess Mama D is right. I will have to teach you a lesson – a lesson you'll never forget."

With that, he cranked the truck, threw it in reverse, and sped back toward Covenant Creek. He was driving faster than before, but the silent trip seemed much longer. Eventually, he turned off the main road and followed an eerie gravel road with trees that overlapped just above the truck and swayed violently in the wind. Since the sun was still not shining, they felt as if they were driving through a long, dark tunnel. Soon, they came to a rusty sign at the end of the road that read "Covenant Creek Cemetery."

Addison grabbed Brennan's hand. "Sir, what kind of lesson is this?" she asked as her voice quivered and a burst of thunder roared loudly then slowly died away.

Life Lessons

"Granddaddy Meek, why did you bring us to an old cemetery to teach us a lesson?" Brennan asked timidly.

Clinging to Brennan, Addison whined, "This is creepy. Does Mom know we're here?"

"Nope," Granddaddy Meek replied as he parked the truck and began getting out. "I'm the oldest person I know. I don't have to ask permission. Now get out and bring that box while you're at it."

They obeyed and hurriedly caught up with him since he had already begun walking through the cemetery without them. Being in the cemetery was bad enough, but such a dark and gloomy day made everything seem much more sinister.

"I don't get why we're in a cemetery. Please tell us what kind of lesson you are trying to teach us," begged Addison.

Granddaddy Meek stopped and glared at them. "Child, I'm teaching you lessons you aren't learning in school. I'm teaching you life lessons."

"But all of these people have died..." Addison said innocently as the thunder continued to rumble.

"I'm proud you know that much!" Granddaddy Meek said sharply. "Look around. See the American flags throughout this cemetery?"

"Yes, sir," both children replied noticing them for the first time.

"Those flags mark the men and women who served in the military," Granddaddy Meek explained. "Many of them gave their lives while in service so that you could live in a free country. This is not just Monday or a holiday for you to celebrate the beginning of summer with a cookout. This Monday is Memorial Day, the one day set aside for our country to honor and remember the bravest in battle."

"Oh," said Addison with surprise, "I didn't know."

"Me either," added Brennan as he hung his head.

Taking the time to look around the entire cemetery and study all the flags dancing in the wind, Addison asked, "How come some of the tombstones with flags look really old and some look new?"

"They're from different wars and different times of service. Come on, I'll show you," he said as he led them toward the very back of the cemetery.

"But, Granddaddy Meek, what if it starts raining on us?" Addison asked worriedly.

"I reckon I'd melt since I'm so sweet," he said sarcastically as he continued to walk unfazed by the noisy thunder and squally winds.

Confused by his serious tone and the thought of him being sweet, Addison stopped, "But I don't want it to rain, Granddaddy Meek. I'm afraid."

"Oh, for Pete's sake, come on," Granddaddy Meek said with frustration. "It's not gonna rain today."

The kids, still uncomfortable with their surroundings and the threatening weather, looked at each other helplessly, then chased after him. Granddaddy Meek was a little on the strange side today; but one thing was for sure, they didn't want to be stranded in the cemetery without him!

Granddaddy Meek finally stopped beside a tall tombstone and leaned against it for support. "This one here is my great-grandfather's oldest brother, my great-uncle Alvin. He was only 18 years old when he was drafted into the Civil War when it began in 1861. Over a year later, he was shot in the leg and soon died."

"Did they get him to a hospital in time?" Addison asked.

"Hardly," Granddaddy Meek said sadly. "If they could have taken him to a hospital, he would have probably lived. But he lay on the battlefield in pain while bullets flew all around him until someone could drag him to safety. They cut his leg off thinking it would save him, but instead it made him worse. He died an agonizing death just like all the soldiers buried right here from the Civil War. They all had big hopes and dreams for their future, but their time was cut short because of war."

"That's awful," Addison whispered as her hair swirled around her face.

"Was your great-grandfather in the Civil War, too?" Brennan asked.

"He sure was. He couldn't wait to serve and be just like his big brother. He joined as soon as he turned eighteen and promised his mother he'd find Alvin. My great-grandfather looked everywhere for him as he went from one battle to the next but was unaware Alvin had already been killed."

"That's sad," Addison said. "I can't imagine how shocked

your great-grandfather must have been when he heard the news."

"Oh, Alvin's death was terribly hard on my great-grandfather," he continued. "He never got over the fact that he made it home and Alvin didn't. He grieved over his brother's death until the day he died. Even as an old man, he'd still cry when he thought about him. He felt like he could have saved him if he had just found him in time."

Granddaddy Meek limped to another tombstone as the children followed closely behind. "This is his tombstone; he was *my* Great-granddaddy Meek. He lived a long life and was a good, God-fearing man. After seeing more death than we can imagine in the Civil War then losing his brother, he made sure to teach his children and grandchildren that freedom is never free. It always comes with a price. What I remember most about him was that he loved God and was never ashamed of it. He cherished his family and was proud of his country despite its many flaws."

The wind seemed to be picking up, and the sky was growing even darker, but it didn't seem to bother Brennan and Addison now that they were captivated by Granddaddy Meek's lessons. Brennan wandered back to examine the older, faded Civil War tombstones with flags for some time. The writing could barely be read and many were even broken. "There sure are a lot of these. How many people actually died in that Civil War?"

"Around 620,000 soldiers," Granddaddy Meek said with a sigh. "That war claimed more lives than any other war in American history. It was especially tragic because we were killing each other."

"How?" Brennan asked wide-eyed.

"You see, the northern states and the southern states of America were battling against each other. Many times, men were fighting their own brothers, cousins, uncles, and sometimes fathers. Women lost husbands; children lost fathers; parents lost children. Our country had drifted far from God, and it resulted in four years of death and devastation."

"Wow, it sounds like it," Brennan agreed.

"Before the war even ended, ladies all over our country would come out to the cemeteries in the spring to place flowers on the many graves of slain Civil War soldiers. They would pray, sing hymns, and grieve the loss of their loved ones killed during that gory war. It was a depressing time for America."

"Did ladies come to this very cemetery?" Addison interrupted.

"You bet they did," he explained. "Nearly every community in the North and the South lost men and even women during the Civil War. After the war ended, the people of Waterloo, New York, closed the whole town down on May 5, 1866, for everyone to decorate the graves of the fallen soldiers with flags and flowers and pay their respects. That gave General John A. Logan the idea to make May 30, 1868, a day to remember the heroes who died in battle. He called that day Decoration Day. He chose that date because no Civil War battle was fought on that particular day and because that was the time of year when flowers would be in bloom."

Addison looked confused, "But didn't you say it was called Memorial Day?"

"I did," Granddaddy Meek continued. "See, the people from the North and the South still didn't get along after the Civil War. Many of them still had very bitter hearts and didn't want to share Decoration Day. However, years later when Americans had no choice but to join and fight together during World War I, it changed people's hearts. When over 100,000 American soldiers were killed in that war, it made the North and the South become more compassionate towards one another and finally unite."

"It's sad that it took more soldiers dying in another war to make the country join together again, but I'm glad they did," Addison said.

"So am I," Granddaddy Meek said. "After that, they decided to rename Decoration Day to Memorial Day. They also decided to honor all soldiers who had lost their lives in any war, dating all the way back to the Revolutionary War. Finally, in 1971, it became an official holiday, and the date was moved from May 30 to the fourth Monday in May. That gave federal workers, like your parents, a day off work to remember the fallen and visit their graves."

"Oh," said Brennan, "I wondered how they got off work every year for our cookout!"

"I hate to admit it, Granddaddy Meek, but we've never visited the graves of soldiers or even known to remember those that died," Addison said with regret.

Granddaddy Meek nodded with sorrow, "You're not the only ones."

"Are there any soldiers from World War I buried here?" Addison asked as leaves blew past her feet.

Granddaddy Meek pointed to another tombstone with a flag wildly flapping. "There are several, but that soldier right there was my fearless Uncle Thomas. He was determined to follow in the footsteps of other courageous men in his family and fight for our country. Like many other young boys his age, he was filled with patriotism. He wanted to be a part of what they thought was a 'Great Adventure.' So, he claimed to be 18 in order to join the war effort, although he was only 16. My grandparents were extremely upset with him for being untruthful and enlisting without their permission."

"That's not much older than I am! I would have been too afraid!" said Brennan.

"Me, too!" Addison added. "What happened to him?"

"He actually died of the flu while overseas. Many people are unaware of this, but far more soldiers serving in World War I died from the flu epidemic than they did in combat. Uncle Thomas' last letter was to his mother telling her of his deathly sickness and asking for her forgiveness. His greatest wish was to be home so she could take care of him."

Addison looked as if she could cry. "I can't imagine being sick in another country, especially during a war! He did need his mother."

"A few months after she was notified of his death, his

mother, who was my grandmother, passed away from a broken heart. My dad was only 12 when he lost his mother *and* brother," Granddaddy Meek said with regret.

As the children let the stories of heroes sink in, they slowly kept walking without saying a word through the rolling thunder and bursts of wind. Then unexpectedly, they heard a loud "CRACK!"

Before they knew it, Brennan and Addison were lying on the ground huddled together, covering their heads from what sounded like a gunshot nearby.

Heavy Stories of History and Heroes

When Addison uncovered her head and looked up, she let out a blood-curdling scream.

"Addison, what is it?" Brennan asked frantically with his eyes closed and his head still covered.

"It's a big, nasty spider!" she squealed, pointing to a web beside her head.

Frustrated, Brennan stood and dusted himself off, "Is that all? I thought we were goners and you're screaming about a spider!"

Granddaddy Meek actually chuckled at the two who were completely overreacting. "You city slickers need to get out more! That spider's not gonna hurt a fly…well, maybe a fly, but not you. He's showing us that even though it feels stormy, it's not gonna rain today."

"How do you know that?" Addison asked still untrusting of the eight-legged enemy.

"My Great-granddaddy Meek and my grandfather were farmers in Covenant Creek. They didn't have the luxury of someone telling them on the TV or the phone what the weather was going to do. They relied on nature. They taught me when I was a boy that if you can't find the spider on his web on a day like this, he's preparing for a storm. If he's resting on the web, he knows it won't rain. That poor spider was relaxing until you scared the living daylights out of him."

"Whoa! I never knew that!" Brennan said. "But wait, the real question is, why in the world was someone shooting at us?"

Granddaddy Meek closed his eyes and shook his head. "Son, no one shot at you! The wind blew down a big limb at the edge of the woods!"

The children couldn't help but laugh at how scared they had been over a silly, old fallen limb.

Trusting Granddaddy Meek's theory about rain and anxious for him to teach them more, they kept searching for flags as the wind beat against them. Brennan spotted another tombstone with a flag close by, "Do you know that man's story?"

"That's not a man," Granddaddy Meek began. "That was a dear sweet lady my grandfather told me stories about. You see, between the Civil War and World War I, America was involved in the Spanish-American War in 1898. It only lasted four months, but a terrible sickness called typhoid fever broke out, and the United States didn't have enough trained people in the military to care for the sick. Much like the flu in World War I, the typhoid fever epidemic was the major killer of Americans during the Spanish-American War.

"Congress allowed the Army to pay female nurses thirty dollars a month to go take care of them. They sent over 1,500 female nurses, and this dear lady was one of them. My grandfather said she loved taking care of people, especially the church people and her children. Her husband had recently been killed in an accident, so she volunteered to serve. Desperate for a way to provide for her family, she promised her little ones she wouldn't be away long and they'd have a better life if she could go and make money for them."

"What happened to her?" Addison asked curiously.

"While taking care of the others, she got sick with the typhoid fever, too," he paused. "But she died a hero."

Addison placed her hand on the tombstone, "Oh, no. She didn't even have to go."

"No, she didn't," Granddaddy Meek said with compassion, "but those women who were willing to serve the sick and injured made their mark in history. Their service was seen as so important that Congress officially allowed women to join the military as nurses from that point forward. Many of those selfless nurses from the Spanish-American War are buried in the Arlington National Cemetery, but it was her wish to be returned to her children in Covenant Creek since she promised to come back home."

"That breaks my heart," Addison said, filled with emotion.

Sorrowfully, Brennan said, "We learn every year in school that people die for our country, but I guess I've never thought about them being real people and having real families."

"Yeah, you're right," Addison added. "We just read about them in textbooks like they are characters in a storybook. Those poor kids waited for their mom to come home and believed they'd have a better life. They lost *both* parents...."

Granddaddy Meek nodded, "That's right. Their lives were forever changed. She loved them more than anything and was willing to give her life, so their lives could be better. That's the same story for everyone out here with a flag. No matter what the situation, their families and their freedoms were worth fighting for."

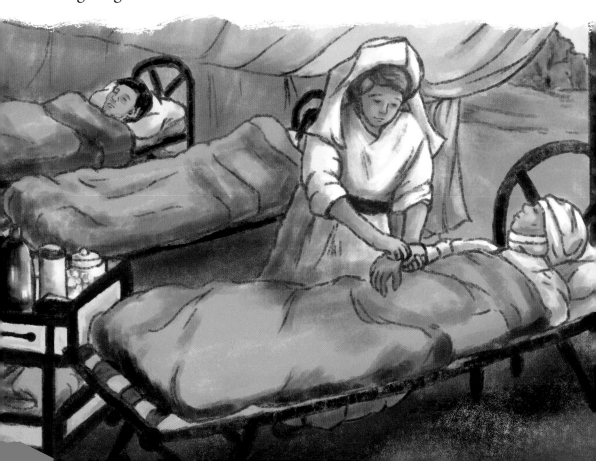

Addison walked away to hide the tears in her eyes. She stopped at another flag and dusted off the tombstone. "Granddaddy Meek, tell me about this one. It says, 'He remains in the hands of Jesus.'"

"Ah, good ol' Jesse," Granddaddy said. "He was a fine young man – always helped others and wanted to make his family proud. He faced many obstacles, but he was actually the very first African American Navy pilot."

"What happened to him?" Brennan asked.

"He and his squadron were sent to the freezing mountains of North Korea in 1950 during the Korean War. He had flown many missions just like that one, but his plane was suddenly shot down. His friend flying a plane beside him saw Jesse's plane fall out of the sky. So, he crashed his plane intentionally and ran to help him, hoping to save him, but Jesse was pinned in the plane. Jesse's last words to his friend were to tell his wife Daisy he loved her."

"Did he have children, too?" Addison asked.

"Just a baby girl who never had the chance to know how heroic her father was and how he changed history. They weren't able to bring his body back home for burial, but they still had a military funeral here. He was given honors for his sacrifice. I'm proud I had the chance to know him."

Distant thunder resounded as the wind nudged Brennan to another nearby tombstone. "Look! This one says POW!"

"P-O-W stands for Prisoner of War," Granddaddy Meek explained as he joined him. "His plane was also shot down, but he was serving in a different war, called Vietnam. He survived the crash, but the enemy found him and held him prisoner. They did horrific things to him, but he refused to betray his country. He was tortured and starved until he finally died.

"When his plane went down, his wife was told he was missing in action, but for years she never knew whether he was dead or alive. She faithfully waited on him and prayed he'd come home. Finally, his body was found and returned to the United States."

"Was he a part of our family?" Addison asked.

Granddaddy Meek shook his head, "No, but he was a part of Covenant Creek. Our whole community mourned with his family and prayed for him after he went missing. His poor wife had to raise three small children by herself, not knowing if he'd

ever come back. I can still remember it like yesterday when the hearse brought his body home."

"Being a prisoner of war must have been a nightmare for him and his family," Brennan said with compassion.

"Oh, it was a nightmare," Granddaddy Meek said. "I remember hanging the first MIA/POW flag at the post office in Covenant Creek in memory of him as soon as they were available after Vietnam. A lady named Mary Hoff, whose husband was also missing in action after his plane was shot down in 1970, pushed for a symbol so those heroes could be remembered. I'm sure you've seen the black and white flag that was created for them. They are flown nationwide today so we'll stop and remember what they went through, along with their families. I never look at one of those flags without thinking of his family."

"Granddaddy Meek," Addison said softly, "after all we've learned, it doesn't feel right to have a big, happy cookout now."

"A cookout is fine, dear, as long as you take time to remember the heroes who became memories in order for you to make memories. I want you to realize that the freedom to have that cookout came at a great price."

"Oh, we do now!" said Brennan. "Will you teach us what we can we do to honor and remember the men and women who gave their lives for our country?"

As the sun began to peek through the clouds and the strong winds settled to a gentle breeze, Granddaddy Meek said, "Sure, you can start by replacing all the old flags with brand new ones. They're under the poppies."

"What are poppies?" Addison asked.

"Poppies are the red flowers in that box we picked up from the VFW," Granddaddy Meek said, pointing to the box.

Brennan's eyes brightened. "Can you tell us any secrets about the VFW?" Brennan asked excitedly.

"Son, I don't know about secrets, but the VFW stands for Veterans of Foreign Wars. It was formed after the Spanish-American War to help soldiers who were returning from war injured or sick from the typhoid fever like we talked about. Its mission since then has been to take care of veterans who have served overseas as well as their families."

"So…does that mean you're not working undercover and there are no animals inside the building?" Brennan asked disappointedly.

Granddaddy Meek stared blankly at Brennan for a while, then shook his head in confusion. "Do you two even know what a veteran is?"

Ashamed, both children shook their heads.

"A veteran is any person who has served in the military, whether they served during war or times of peace."

"I was almost right!" Brennan snickered as he looked at Addison. "She thought veterans had something to do with animals!"

Granddaddy Meek looked hopeless for a moment but pressed on. "Anyway, as I was saying, one way the VFW helps veterans and their families now is by selling these poppies.

"Back during World War I, a beautiful countryside in Western Europe was completely destroyed by the blasts of battle. It became an ugly, muddy spot where hundreds of soldiers were buried. On May 3, 1915, a Canadian doctor and poet, Lieutenant Colonel John McCrae, sat in that field on the back of an ambulance staring at his friend's grave who had been killed in battle the day before. Everything surrounding him looked dull and depressing, but he began to notice the little red poppies growing all around the white crosses that marked the graves. In memory of his friend, he took a few moments and wrote the world's most famous war poem in history. That poem, 'In Flanders Fields,' is still read at Memorial Day ceremonies today."

"I've heard of that poem!" said Brennan.

"Good!" said Granddaddy Meek, "It's a great poem. It moved

the heart of an American teacher named Moina Michael and inspired her to write her own poem in response to McCrae's called 'We Shall Keep the Faith.' But she didn't stop there, she was determined to make the poppy a national symbol of remembrance for veterans. As she began to make silk poppies and sell them in order to raise money for veterans coming home from World War I, she became known as the 'Poppy Lady.' Her hard work paid off because the poppy is still the symbol today for remembering the lives lost in battle. It's the official memorial flower of the VFW as well."

"That's why the VFW you took us to had a flower shop inside!" Addison exclaimed.

"No, there's no flower shop inside," Granddaddy Meek said patiently. "These poppies are made by disabled veterans through the Buddy Poppy Program, which began in 1924 to support veterans and their families."

"So, real warriors who've been hurt or sick made these?" Brennan asked in amazement.

"That's right," said Granddaddy Meek. "My mother and grandmothers strongly believed in decorating the graves of soldiers on Memorial Day like the ladies we talked about earlier. I promised them I'd carry on their tradition. They normally just placed flowers from their gardens on the graves of the fallen, but actually, on Memorial Day, we should remember all veterans in the cemetery who have passed away.

"I honor them by replacing the old flags from the year before with new ones. Instead of using fresh flowers, I prefer to attach a poppy to the flags of the heroes who sacrificed their lives while in service. This sets them apart and also helps to support the disabled veterans who made the poppies."

"That's really cool, Granddaddy Meek," said Addison, "I've never known about any of this. I'm glad we came here today."

"You two go ahead and replace all the flags you see. Pay special attention to the flags that have old poppies attached and make sure you put out new ones. Take time to consider that every veteran tombstone represents a real soldier with a real story," Granddaddy Meek instructed.

"Yes, sir," the siblings replied as they began their mission.

Once their job was finally completed, they looked around for Granddaddy Meek to tell him they were finished…but he was gone.

A Weeping Warrior

Panic set in as heavy clouds covered the sun once more and darkened the cemetery. A peculiar wind whisked around them, sending chill bumps down their necks as they immediately began to search for Granddaddy Meek. However, he was nowhere to be found. "What could've happened to him?" Brennan asked.

"I don't know, but I'm worried!" Addison said.

Suddenly, they heard crying but saw no sign of him. Afraid he was hurt, they frantically began to run and call his name. Finally, they found him on his knees with his hand on a unique tombstone. "Granddaddy Meek, are you ok?" Brennan asked breathlessly.

Wiping tears from his red eyes, he answered, "I'm fine, son. This is just a tough day. Brings back a lot of memories."

Addison knelt beside Granddaddy Meek and wrapped her arm around his. Realizing the tombstone had a picture on it, she quietly said, "That's the same man from the picture in the kitchen."

"He was my best friend," Granddaddy Meek said as a sob slipped out.

Brennan placed his hand on his back, "What happened to him?"

"We grew up together, went through all our years of training together, and had big plans. James was like a brother to me." Granddaddy Meek paused as his chin quivered and tears spilled down his face. "We were sent to serve in Iwo Jima during World War II. It was supposed to be a quick, easy mission, but it turned into a nightmare before we ever stepped on the beach. They were firing at us from every direction, and we couldn't even see them."

"Who was?" Brennan asked curiously.

"The Japanese," he replied sniffling. "We never dreamed they were hiding in the volcano on the island and in miles of underground tunnels. As our Higgins boat floated to the beach and the door let down, we looked at each other one more time. We had promised to stay right beside each other to protect one another, but as soon as we stepped into the water to run toward the beach, he went under and never came up. I couldn't go back for him. I had orders to keep going. I've tried my best to forget, but some things just won't go away." Granddaddy Meek began to weep, "I just wanted to save him."

Tears fell down Addison's cheek, too, as she leaned in to hug Granddaddy Meek. "I'm so sorry," she said as she hugged him even tighter, "But, I'm glad you came home."

"I am, too," added Brennan. "Thank you for your service, Granddaddy Meek. Aren't we supposed to honor you today since you served, too?"

"No, sir," Granddaddy Meek said firmly, wiping tears with his handkerchief. "Veterans Day is for remembering all service men and women, but Memorial Day is for the real heroes… like James."

It wasn't easy for them to see a mighty man like Granddaddy Meek cry. For the first time ever, they truly understood the significance of Memorial Day and what it means to remember the fallen.

Kneeling to hug him, Brennan said, "Thank you for being patient with us as you teach us. I see why you were upset with us this morning. I'm sorry for being disrespectful, and I'll never think of this day as just a holiday to celebrate summer again."

With a trembling voice, Granddaddy Meek said, "I'm sorry for my bad attitude and for losing my temper this morning, too. I'm not upset with you. It just hurts to feel like no one cares or remembers Memorial Day. Just promise me that you'll remember these brave warriors and carry on this tradition with your children."

"We'd be happy to," said Brennan.

With watery eyes, Addison pulled up the old flag at Granddaddy Meek's dear friend's tombstone and pushed a new one into the ground. Brennan began to respectfully pin a poppy on the flag stem when Granddaddy Meek suddenly grabbed his arm. "No," he said abruptly, "he doesn't get a poppy. Head to the truck. It's time to go."

Families of the Fallen

Brennan and Addison couldn't fathom why Granddaddy Meek wouldn't let them give his friend a poppy and why he rushed to leave, but they didn't question. Without saying a word, they followed him to the truck, still thinking of all they had learned. Everyone remained silent as they traveled down the curvy roads with potholes until finally, Granddaddy Meek pulled in the driveway of a small wooden house.

"Addison, you take the pie Mama D made, and Brennan, you grab a poppy," Granddaddy Meek said.

Again, they did as they were told and followed him to the doorsteps of the house. He knocked and patiently waited. A sweet, elderly lady answered the door with a smile, "Hello,

Dennis. I was looking for you to come by but didn't know if you'd be out in this weather today."

As they hugged each other, they both sniffled and wiped tears from their faces. "Who do you have with you?" she asked.

"These are my great-grandchildren, Brennan and Addison. They're staying with us for the summer," he replied as he proudly looked at them.

"How lovely," she said smiling. "What a blessing. I'm sure you are teaching them well."

"I'm trying," he said putting his hand on Brennan's shoulder. "This gentleman has something for you, Mary."

Shyly, Brennan handed her the poppy. As she took it from him, she wiped a few more tears and said, "My James would be happy to meet you. He sure loved your great-grandfather. You favor Dennis when he was young."

Brennan swelled with pride. "Thank you. And I also want to thank you for your and Mr. James' sacrifice. I wish I could have known him."

"Me, too," Addison added. "We promise to never forget him." Addison hugged her and handed her the pie from Mama D.

Granddaddy Meek smiled and tipped his hat at Mrs. Mary, "We're here if you need us."

"Thank you again for stopping by, and it was nice to meet you, children," she said as they all waved and walked back to the truck.

Once Granddaddy Meek began driving, Addison couldn't

hold her question any longer. "How come we didn't leave Mr. James a poppy?"

"James and I promised each other on the ship before we went into battle that we would take care of each other's wives if one of us didn't make it home. We wanted to make sure our wives always had flowers to enjoy while they lived. Even though these aren't real, it's the thought that counts and the act of remembering."

"How romantic," Addison said, holding her heart.

"Plus," Granddaddy Meek continued, "she will visit him later. She grows special flowers just for him on Memorial Day."

"That's some kind of love," Brennan said with amazement.

Granddaddy Meek motioned toward the box. "There are some extra poppies in that box. Not only can you use them to decorate the graves of soldiers, you're also supposed to wear them in memory of the soldiers and to remind others of their bravery and sacrifice."

"We can have one?" Addison asked excitedly.

"Sure. Hurry and put them on the left side of your shirt. We have one more stop to make."

Just as Brennan and Addison pinned their poppies on, they pulled into another driveway. The house looked more modern than Mrs. Mary's.

"Come on," Granddaddy Meek said. "Grab the other pie and the last poppies."

Once they were all on the porch, Granddaddy Meek knocked on the door. A sad-looking boy their age opened the door, "Hi, Mr. Meek."

"Hey there, J.D., is your mom home?" Granddaddy Meek asked.

Brennan and Addison were surprised Granddaddy Meek knew this boy and that they actually seemed to be friends. His mom appeared behind him and though she seemed sad too, she smiled when she saw them. "Mr. Meek, we sure appreciate you stopping by, especially on such a dark and gloomy day."

"Well, the weather is no bother; it just expresses how we feel on this day," Granddaddy replied.

"It sure does," she agreed. "But God's mercies are new every morning, and the sun will shine again!"

"You're exactly right," Granddaddy Meek said knowingly. "My great-grandchildren and I came to deliver Mama D's pie

and your poppies and tell you how much we appreciate your husband's service and sacrifice to our country. I wish I could have known him. I know he'd be right proud of you and J.D. If there's anything we can do, please don't hesitate to call."

Tears poured down the lady's face. "Thank you for remembering him, Mr. Meek. To everyone else, life has gone on, but we still miss him and need him every day."

"I know you do…and you always will," Granddaddy Meek said as he hugged her the last time and said goodbye.

On the way to the truck, Brennan whispered, "That boy's dad was killed in war?"

Granddaddy Meek nodded with remorse, "He was killed last year by a roadside bomb in Iraq. They just moved here a few months ago to be closer to their family. Poor J.D. sure is struggling."

Brennan glanced back at J.D. sitting alone on the porch holding a football. "He has no one to throw the football with. Can I invite him over to play a while?"

"That sounds like a plan that would make his father proud," Granddaddy Meek said with a smile.

A Moment to Remember

The old pickup truck was filled with laughter as they arrived back at Granddaddy Meek and Mama D's house in time for lunch. J.D. noticed the flag before they even got out of the truck. "Hey, you remembered!"

"Remembered what?" Brennan asked curiously.

"Mr. Meek remembered to fly the flag at half-staff on Memorial Day. My dad taught me that," J.D. said proudly.

"Did he teach you when to raise the flag back up?" Granddaddy Meek asked.

"Yes, sir," J.D. answered confidently. "It's supposed to be raised at 12:00 and stay there until sunset."

Granddaddy Meek smiled, "Your father did a fine job teaching you, young man. It's almost noon, so you're welcome to raise that flag and teach your friends how while you're at it. When you are finished, come on in the house. Mama D will have lunch ready."

"I'll be glad to, but if it starts to rain, I'll take it down. I know the flag isn't supposed to be out in bad weather," J.D. said respectfully.

"Don't worry," Brennan said, pulling J.D. towards the flagpole. "Granddaddy Meek and the spiders know there's no rain in the forecast today!"

Granddaddy Meek chuckled as he watched them from the front porch. He couldn't believe the city kids were actually learning and enjoying the ways of the country. Unlike Mama D, he had not been a bit pleased with the arrangement to keep two overly talkative, energetic children at his age. For the last week, they had completely disrupted his peaceful routines, but he realized Mama D was right. They did need a teacher. He was no longer built for battle, but this was a mission he felt sure he was called to complete, even if they did drive him crazy most of the time.

After lunch, Brennan and Addison introduced J.D. to the farm animals and showed him their fort in the old barn. They splashed through the creek, played hide-and-seek, and then threw the football until Granddaddy Meek and Mama D walked out to the front yard where they were playing and asked them to come to the flag.

"Is everything okay?" Brennan asked, panting from playing hard.

"Everything's fine, dear," Mama D replied.

As they gathered around the flagpole with the flag now flying high, Granddaddy Meek began, "This is another important tradition I'd like for you to start now and continue with your own children and grandchildren one day. Most Americans don't know this, but Congress established a Moment of Remembrance in 2000 for the veterans who gave their lives while serving our country. Our society is normally too busy focusing on the Memorial Day celebrations, but we are supposed to stop what we are doing a few minutes before three o'clock and be silent for one minute while we remember their sacrifice. They paid the ultimate price for us, so we need to be willing to spare at least one minute to honor them."

With a shaky voice, J.D. said, "My dad and I would always listen to 'Taps' during the Moment of Remembrance. Even though it's painful to listen to because it was played at his funeral, nothing makes me feel more proud of my dad and my country."

"I understand, son," Granddaddy Meek agreed.

At exactly three o'clock, the five of them bowed their heads as Granddaddy Meek recited Psalm 23, written by another great warrior, King David. While a few cars passed them on the highway and the sky remained dim, J.D. prayed, followed by Granddaddy Meek. Then they all remained silent to honor the American heroes from the Revolutionary War to our present-day wars.

A Shared Celebration

After a few more hours of playing outside, the children ran to the kitchen for Mama D's famous sweet potato pie. They were all too busy laughing and sharing stories to even notice when Mom and Dad walked in.

"Hey, kiddos, we're back! Are you ready to go?" Dad asked.

"Awe, do we have to go already?" Addison grumbled.

Mom looked shocked. "You've been here all day! Don't you remember what today is?"

Brennan smiled, "We sure do!"

"It's Memorial Day!" Addison proclaimed. "All this time we just thought we celebrated this day because it was the beginning of summer, but Granddaddy Meek taught us a lesson in a cemetery we will never forget!"

Mom's eyes shamefully fell to the floor, "I remember him taking me to the cemetery when I was a girl. I placed poppies and flags on the tombstones with him every year, and I always loved visiting Mr. James' wife. I'm sorry for not teaching you guys and taking time to remember our heroes. Your dad and I got too busy over the years and forgot to be thankful for the ones who died so that we could live this beautiful, busy life. So, you know what?"

"What?" asked Brennan, not knowing what to expect.

Mom smiled, "I think we should invite J.D. and his family, Mr. James' wife, Granddaddy Meek, and Mama D to our cookout! We can celebrate family and freedom together and honor Mr. James and J.D.'s dad, along with the other great American heroes."

"Yes!" shouted the boys.

"That sounds wonderful," said Mama D.

J.D. was smiling from ear to ear as he said, "I can't wait! Today may still be dark and cloudy outside, but this is the brightest I have felt in a long time!"

"Thank you, Mom and Dad!" shouted Addison who ran to tell Granddaddy Meek.

However, before she opened the front door, she peered at him on the porch through the window. He was sitting in his chair holding the picture of Mr. James. Though she was excited about the cookout, her heart ached for the pain Granddaddy Meek had experienced in losing his friend. As she watched him study the picture, she remembered something he had told her on the first day she spent in Covenant Creek.

"Simper Fidelis," he had told her, "that means 'always faithful.'"

Focusing on him from the window, she couldn't help but think of how he reminded her of the spider in the cemetery. Just like the spider leaves the web when he knows bad weather is coming, Granddaddy Meek had left his home to protect his country when the storms of war came. But, much like the spider calmly enjoying his web today, Granddaddy Meek can now also securely rest in his peaceful home because of his service and the sacrifice of true American heroes.

Addison had never even heard of Simper Fidelis before she came to Covenant Creek, but thankfully, she had truly learned what it looks like to always be faithful just by watching Granddaddy Meek. Like his great-grandfather, he too had been faithful to God, his family, and even his friend and fellow Marine, Mr. James, whom he still cherished so many years later.

Addison was thankful for her heritage. Her wise Great-granddaddy Meek had been taught well, and now he was passing on what he had learned. Her heart filled with gratefulness as she understood for the first time just how blessed she really was.

ISBN: 978-1-935932-12-3

AMERICAN FAMILY ASSOCIATION
PO Drawer 2440
Tupelo, Mississippi 38803
www.afa.net

Printed in the United States of America
Signature Book Printing, www.sbpbooks.com

This book is available at **afastore.net** or by calling 662-844-5036.

Produced by Canada Burns
Designed by Canada Burns
Edited by Joy Lucius